Seeking Self

Barbara Gurney
Seeking Self

Seeking Self
ISBN 978 1 76109 029 5
Copyright © text Barbara Gurney 2020
Cover: Lorri Lennox

First published 2020 by
GINNINDERRA PRESS
PO Box 3461 Port Adelaide 5015
www.ginninderrapress.com.au

Contents

Declaration of Soul	7
Shrink Not	8
Forest	9
The Dove	10
Hello Again	12
After the Film	13
A New Treasure	14
The Deceit of Beauty	15
When There's a Moment	16
A Forever Evening	17
And the Pipers Played…	18
Come Back to Me	19
At the Corner	20
Palette Bold	21
Road to Nowhere	22
Cornerstone 1	23
Cornerstone 2	24
Cornerstone 3	25
The Tourist's Curse	26
Riverside	27
The Poacher	28
Beyond Everyday	29
Celebrate the Now	30
Music Explosion	31
Strzelecki's Mountain	32
Clickety Clackety Track	33
Waiting for Yesterday	34
I Remember	35
Sometimes It Only Takes a Smile	36
Of Trees	37

Convict	38
Depths	39
Touching the Soul of Fashion	40
Electronic Power	41
Gentle Day	42
Homeless	43
When Leaves Fall	44
Emma's Memories	46
Fallen Petals	47
Feelings	48
Cherries	50
The Plains of Lebanon	51
Forever	52
Algae	53
I Am Glass	54
Proud	55
Worthless	56
Graveside	57
I Saw Beauty	58
Silence of Love	59
I'm Here	60
Let Go	62
Water	63
Lucifer of Hate	64
Noisy Contemplation	65
Colour Me Black	66
Beyond Remorse	67
One Soul	68
Rodeo Riding	70
The Old Woman	71
Yesterday and You	72
Whispering Hope	73
Shadow of Me	74

Declaration of Soul

In the centre of where I truly am
I soar above clouds with egotistical applause
Yet sink like a stone on water of rejection
Contented days
Poignant days
With truth
And lies
Revealing nothing
Knowledge of self
Exposed to only me

Shrink Not

In a slip of time
In a speck of a moment
Life can change
Life will change

Looking back and valuing those moments

Or maybe…

Did the future suffer from
    an inopportune raised eyebrow
    a shrug of impatience
    an unanswered phone call

Could the future have been altered
    with a softer word
    a gentle hand on a shoulder
    an encouraging smile

However
    regret conquers
    brings passion to its knees
    brings hope, dreams, desires undone

Therefore
    shrink not from your past decisions

Instead
    change the future

Forest

They stand tall
Black
Bare
Tortured by flame
Losing much
But winning
In the struggle against fate

We wait for renewal

The Dove

Shockwaves strike the dove
Its feathers tremble
For a millisecond the air is astonishingly quiet

Learning is spewed from frantic minds
Algebra changes
X becomes real
A body previously soaking up Shakespeare now puddles with blood as it inhabits the floor
Feet trample the panic of safety
Eyes wide with shock
    – of one person's disregard for their tomorrow

The dove wants those below to:
    learn
    expand
    fill their dreams and desires
to be who they can be
in a world of wonderment and satisfaction

Sirens scream like children
Children scream like tracer bullets
Huddling with friends
    glad to be alive
    sad to be alive
When it only takes one madman to take so much

The dove trembles
Moves along the knotty branch
Peeks out from behind withering leaves
Its daily rituals ruined by
    frantic movement
    sobbing
    sirens…sirens…
    screams…screams…

One-sided conversations of hysterical pleading
Students begging for security
Unknown saviours clutch trembling bodies

Silent, bullet-laden heroes lay where destiny struck
No longer in pain
No longer…

The survivors remain crouched
Bent in anger
Until they demand to be heard

They rally
They scream once again

Let us learn in peace

The dove flies away

Hello Again

Hand in hand we wander
Through drifts of Paterson's curse
Across long grasses under bud-filled gums

We soar to far off places
Of steeples, castles, dungeons
Of pretty stained-glass windows

Amid crowds, umbrella following
We see brass plaques with shine attended
Statues heralding tales re-told
Cobbled paths echoing unknown steps
Ancient stories hiding truths
History in a moment lost

Seaside pauses near wind-blown palms
Cold waters around our toes
We're immersed in tropical glee

Pyramids and rivers blue
Beside foreign words and customs
Beneath the heat of our sun-filled days

Far off lands shared in a glow
No ache or pain to claim us
Only smiles and welcome calm

As slumber leaves
This dream has brought you back to me

After the Film

'I didn't know I could be so scared,'
    said the young woman on the screen.

In the after-quietness, I could only imagine:

> *Fear building*
> *Courage struggling*
> *As the Red Peril fly low*
> *Repeating their premeditated attack*
> *Taking away lives amid a blazing Darwin*
> *The Post Office – nothing left to send*
>
> *Teapots and teacups rattling to breaking point*
> *Books and pencils scattering*
> *Desks tipping into rubble*
>
> *Children terrified*
> *Adults baffled*
> *Soldiers puzzled*
> *Seaman confused*

Then:

Poignant stillness captures our respect
Our feet tread organised paths of history
Beneath fragrant frangipani blooms

Lest We Forget

A New Treasure

Deep in the forest where man fells a tree
The heart of nature wonders how it can be
But out of destruction someone works with a lathe
Turning and polishing, delighting the heart once again

The Deceit of Beauty

Age defied in the lens
A tilt of elegance
Dark lashes entice desire

Beneath are lies
Hidden in a tender heart

Look upon the loveliness with sadness
Have mercy for the beautiful shell
For the inner soul is broken

When There's a Moment

After the storm:
>Not now
>While there's hair-flattening wind
>While feet-chilling puddles hinder the way

After the storm:
>Not now
>While frantic dashes under uncooperative umbrellas are suffered
>While fear of thunder and fright of lightning is foremost

After the storm:
>Now
>With a toasty-warm mug thawing still hands
>When flaming logs scare chilblains away

After the storm:
>Now
>When the ruined day is over
>When chores are done and comfort reigns

After the storm:
>Now
>When thoughts are calm
>When I can think of you

A Forever Evening

like a wave lapping the shore
      calm
      savoured

like a breeze through treetops
      serene
      uplifting

like a wag from man's best friend
      companionable
      dependable

like a softening sunset
      promising
      eternal

And the Pipers Played…

Written with a memory of nightfall's entreaty
Each note a heartfelt message
Composed with a plea:
> Ease the world's conflicts
> Have hate disappear
> Bring music to suffering souls
> Love for those in need
> Even for just this moment

Each note upon the chanter
Telling of hope on dancing fingers
The lingering melody
Blending harmonies
Spine-tingling perfection
Reaching the power of the day

But drummers cause a memory
Of evil and destruction
Of wars destroying peace

One million listening ears
Wanted the dream to call the tune
And as the crowd applauded
The pipers played…
'I Dreamed There Was No War'

Come Back to Me

I'll forgive the thunder you stormed
    the lightning
        struck as all-consuming power

grasp life and start again
tumble down memories of better days
as the stars sigh and moonbeams cry
let broken pieces fall as rain
going from separation
into a new sharing

At the Corner

I stand at the corner and look longingly beyond

    Beyond the concrete footpath
    Beyond the tarmac road

    Where there used to be a river
    Where there used to be a park

I stand at the corner and look longingly beyond

    Beyond the shopping centre
    Beyond the countless cars

    Where there used to be some wattles
    Where there used to be some gum trees

I stand at the corner and look longingly beyond

    Beyond man's need for progress
    Beyond man's need for recognition

    When there used to be pride in flora
    When there used to be pride in fauna

I stand at the corner

    Bereaved of what we gave away
    Of what we should have known

Palette Bold

Exotic flare of colour
Painted on each flamingo
Worn with a show of accomplished pride
Feather soft
Palette bold

Mass adornment owned by them
From stately head to exuberant wing
Shocking the unadorned world
Feather soft
Palette bold

A flock of faultless opulence
Viewed with awe and wonder
Making envy no part of lust
Feather soft
Palette bold

Put aside futile comparison
Accept nature's beauty
Absorb the splendour in equal part
Feather soft
Palette bold

Road to Nowhere

Somewhere in the mist of memory
Somewhere where my heart once lived
    A road led me to you

Amongst the fresh-faced flush of youth
Amongst a plan of a forever
    A road beckoned on

Beside flowers of paired contentment
Beside blossoms of wedded bliss
    A road turned corners

Because pain became your struggle
Because tragedy encompassed me
    A road became a detour

When my soul broke from your passing
When loneliness covered my all
    A road became less travelled

Somewhere in the mist of memory
Somewhere while my heart lives empty
    That road leads to nowhere

Cornerstone 1

Is not the cornerstone only one part of the whole?
Resolute in guarding weakness
Relying on solid formation

Is not the cornerstone only one part of the whole?
Surrounded by those loaning their power
Strengthened together

Cornerstone 2

Are you strong enough to stand?
When the cornerstone crumbles
Shocked at rejection
The pain of insidious tampering
Biting into the stone

Charade of fantasy
A sham of useless attention

Are you strong enough to stand?
When I no longer can
Drained by impulse
Of shattered caring
Diminishing the stone

Ignored with pretence
And meaningful deception

Are you strong enough to stand?
Without sustenance
Bled from your source
Never acknowledged
Emptying the stone

Are you strong enough to stand?

Cornerstone 3

Can I bear their expectations?
Their ability to shrug away the responsibilities
Thrust then upon me

I too am weak

Can I bear my expectations?
My want to pander
Spoilt, by indulgence

Together we can be strong

The Tourist's Curse

Ancient buildings stand proud
While encumbered umbrellas demand obedience
As diverse words spill in momentary awe

Do walls crumble with repugnance as cameras click
Do cobblestones tremble beneath feet from many shores

Is homage lost for boast
With wonder left on technology
And souvenirs hidden by dust and disregard

Is history dishonoured by indifference

Riverside

I see nature at her best:

Mulch of yesterday's life
   new shoots of tomorrow's promise
      hollows and hidey-holes for the timid
         fields of grass for the bold

Silver reflections caress the water
   dancing as clouds edge out the sun
      brushed peppermint leaves' fragrance lingers
         crisp air heightens mindfulness

My feet follow the winding path
I breathe in calmness
acknowledge tranquillity
and leave with heart-filled awe

The Poacher

His brow is deep
With saddened eyes
Like trampled rabbit burrows
Of sodden fields
Whose joy has fled
From youthful heart

Beyond Everyday

I want to float around diamonds in inky skies
Grasp moonbeams; let them squiggle over my palms

Be there
Not here
In the ordinary

Reach beyond routine
Touch excitement
Colour my world with one more clutch of change

Celebrate the Now

Expectations rang loud like the bells of St Martin's
Darted and sang as if a bird through a tree
Ability ran, chased goals idealistic
Lay sleeping with dreams unencumbered

Ah, glorious youth
but now it is gone

The mirror reflects an image surrendering to time
Scribbled across cheeks are the journeys of life
An uncompliant body yearns for motion
Bending under the soul of remembrance

Hope now competes with stark reality
Hiding behind fear like the sun behind clouds
In a garden of memory
Wilted roses echo the existence of age

Ah, glorious maturity
for here it is

Time to challenge like an unfaltering warrior
Brave in attempting concepts anew
Brush aside notions of failure and pride
Press forward to new potentials

Some lose the chance to become mellow
For many the path is muddy and tiresome
Be one who steps eagerly awaiting adventure
Shines, like the stars on a clear night's sky

Ah, glorious day
celebrate the now

Music Explosion

Crash! – a symbol strikes
    quavers leap from the stave
        attacks with frenzy
ebony and ivory assaults
    molests the mind
        dares recognition
trumpet and percussion
    reverberates through veins
        tells its story then settles
infusing melodies known
    a familiar blanket of joy
        with warmth and depth of tones
sweet jewels of melodies linger
    transporting Vienna and maestros
        violins and oboes
rhythms soften to a heart-beating waltz
    harmonies embrace
        Dance! it tells me

Strzelecki's Mountain

Water tumbles over stones beneath pygmy possum's paws
After a glance at the sky, it scrambles to safety

Far off, above the windblown slopes
a wedge-tailed eagle watches the marsupial disappear
the hungry raptor drops
then rises
barely moving its elegant wings
waiting patiently
flies across scrubby mountain top
down into the valley,
lands on a solitary snow gum
sits motionless
a snake warms its belly on the roadside
sensing footsteps, slithers beneath the concrete walkway

A human tide strides up a convenient metal platform
The height needs conquering
Achievement will be cherished
Few notice puddles left by last night's rain
Fewer admire yellow dots of the Billy Button flowers
One lifts their eyes and watches the eagle soar once more

Clickity Clackity Track

Life is a journey
    with stops and starts
        with spectacular surprises

OR

A path to well-planned every day
    with predictable programs
        with tortuous timelines
            with drudge and drear

NO!

Take the clickety clackety track
    towards an exuberant existence
        towards the unexpected and unknown

With the joy of
    another station
        another platform

On the clickety clackety track

Waiting for Yesterday

He doesn't beg
Just waits

Behind solid bars of confinement
On cold floors of rejection
Wondering what he has done
Or hasn't

He wants to run with frolicking children
Yap when the key goes in the lock
Chase magpies without intention
Take titbits from hands dangling below the table
Curl up on a couch –
    one paw on his human

Like he did

But for now,
Without begging
he waits

I Remember

I remember, said the grandfather

What do you remember? asked the boy

Marching comes easy
The other stuff, bit harder

What else do you remember? asked the boy

Little and some more
More and too much

What else do you remember? asked the boy

Days turning to night
Night becoming another bloody day

What else do you remember? asked the boy

Buildings blown up
Towns destroyed

What else do you remember? asked the boy

Fellow soldiers becoming mates
Sharing the pain and loss

What else do you remember? asked the boy

I don't want to remember the rest, said the grandfather

Sometimes It Only Takes a Smile

I couldn't laugh, there was no way
I frowned and scowled, refused to play
My sadness felt it's here to stay

I walked along a nearby street
I saw the path, I saw my feet
My frown it deepened in repeat

I saw a man as I walked a mile
He stopped by me, we talked a while
And when he left, I wore a smile

Of Trees

Of twisted bark
Of hidden ants
Trees majestic in their stand

Of fateful imports
Of local gums
Trees majestic in their stand

Of glorious colour
Of scented leaves
Trees majestic in their stand

Of mankind's need
Of nature's call
Trees majestic in their stand

Convict

Convict
Poor, desperate
Starving, struggling, stealing
Unable to get ahead
Prisoner

Convict
Chained, abused
Suffering, yielding, battling
Trying to get ahead
Felon

Convict
Pardoned, freeman
Building, planting, succeeding
Seeing the way ahead
Australian

Depths

In the depths of a forest where trees stand straight and tall
A wandering joey fears no one
A magpie warbles his song

In the depths of a forest where grass is teased by wind
A kookaburra's laugh echoes
A bobtail hides in fallen leaves

At the edge of a forest where trees are felled by man
A kangaroo leaves his homeland
A dugite's life has gone

At the edge of a forest where chainsaws fill the air
A dove has lost its nesting home
An orchid will bloom no more

In the depths of our hearts where we long for peace and calm
An understanding of man's requirements
A knowing that progress prowls

In the depths of our hearts where tender moments rise
A longing for the yesterday
A desire for harmony for all

Touching the Soul of Fashion

Scissors, patterns, tape measures, satin, lace, pins, thread, needles, fittings, finishes…

Beyond the glamour
Beneath chic trends
Under sensuous skin
Is the human core

Fashion brings with it:
    A countenance of style
    Shaking a fist at comparisons
    With light-footed steps of pleasure
    Beyond the ordinary
    To confidence

Glitter

Glamour

Catwalk

Photographs

Applause

Electronic Power

Crumpled heart
From electronic words
Tormented by keystrokes
Tap, tap

Vicious words won't be deleted
From a vulnerable memory
As they're saved in an unwanted acceptance
Tap, tap

Send
Receive
Cruel accusations
Absolute lies
Tap, tap

Words sit on a silent screen
Crashing through thoughts
Straight to the soul
With electronic power
Tap, tap

☺

Tap, tap
Silence

Gentle Day

like a wave lapping the shore
    calm
    savoured

like a breeze through treetops
perfume from a garden
    serene
    uplifting

like a blanket across the shoulders
a smile from a friend
    cosy
    sincere

Homeless

Winter closing and summer welcomes
Dread departing the dank and dreary dark

Cool breezes across lapping river edges
Eucalyptus aromas scenting the day
Glow of the eastern dawning
Wandering souls leave guardian bridges

But where do they leave their coats?

When Leaves Fall

Leaves fall from trees
Like the joy from my heart
Those leaves will turn to other forms
And I too will be forever changed

My tears come freely
Because you have gone
our time is o'er
And I am alone

I remember our first meeting
And the path we travelled
Together we journeyed
Made stories untold

I remember our children
Of our face and our teachings
Their achievements
Our pride

I remember family
Some gone, some far
Of those near in place
Near in heart

I remember times
When achievement and laughter
Filled corners and took away sadness
Brought happiness once more

But now, the lost love scatters
Like mulch on the ground
Touching the new growth
Of the years still to come

Leaves will stop falling
When spring brings life
And my tears may one day ease
But our memories will forever be

Emma's Memories

Long tales of founding days
    When jarrah was felled
    And new ground plowed

Long tales of struggling days
    When hands worked raw
    And arms leathered from sun

Long tales of hardship days
    When dams were dry
    And trees stood bare

Long tales of happy days
    When love was strong
    And children laughed loud

Long tales of fruitful days
    When citrus grew quick
    And sales were bold

Long tales of joyous days
    When family expanded
    And hearts were full

These tales of this your life
    I will pen for you
    For I remember well

Fallen Petals

Beyond the picket fence lie wistful dreams of bygone days

    When petunias danced
    And daffodils pranced

When hours of toil turned to vistas of pleasure

Before knees no longer bend and fingers no longer grip
Behind a tangle of rye grass
Hidden in a turmoil of dandelions

    Petunias are cursed
    But daffodils still burst

Beyond the picket fence where the dream lingered until reality came

Feelings

I am what I feel

Soft melancholy moods of evening
nights of gripping longing
awakening to the dew of pain amid loving splendour

Tender moments of self
    becoming proud
    wanting adulation

Quick breath of desire for pastures greener than owned

Trembling against threatening misery
    of solitude
    of aged tremors hiding stale memories

feeling
    with each day
    a little more
    than deserved

feeling
    with each day
    a little less
    than deserved

Am I other than a feeling?

Visions indulge sighted decadence
Bound words offer knowledge
The wound of picked roses
      ignored by encumbered fragrance
Every note from an enchanted scale
      heard

But these senses return to my soul
      making me feel
      making me feel

Cherries

A cherry on top, she asks

A treat with extras, I ponder

Like
    a lingering hug
    a smile radiating from eyes
    life, with tinsel and baubles

A cherry on top, she asks again

Doesn't everyone want that cherry on life
    a garden with endless flowers
    a purse always full
    friends forever near

My mind turns

Consider a final topping
    on sorrow
    on pain
    on toil

Would
    love be deeper for experiencing loss
    gain be appreciated after struggle
    sunshine be more treasured through stormy clouds

I pause
    yes, I answer
    this time I'll have the cherry

The Plains of Lebanon

A bitter land
Where the sun beats forever
Tiptoeing lizards pant their journey
Human footprints distorted, then gone
Scorched winds toss tent corners
Where the burden for man is survival

Forever

I don't know if I've told you
Of expectations fallen short
How once I thought *I do* didn't necessarily mean forever

A tall dark handsome silhouette hovered
Leaned in and whispered greetings
My desire at once became captured
And the temptation wouldn't leave

In the darkness of the night
No moon to show our meeting
I tucked away *forsaking all others* and returned his enticing smile

His hello turned to murmurings
I took them all on board
I even forgot about *till death doth part*
Until he touched my cheek

This man of shadows wouldn't be forever
Only an encounter which would depart
Then my promise masked the lust and I turned towards the light
And left the tall dark handsome one
Drove back home to honour my pledge
Forever

Algae

Mud oozes between my toes
I slip, grab at the reeds
This used to be clear water
A fishing paradise
Now the algae clings
And my heart bleeds

I Am Glass

Strong when flames flick and burn
But shattered in a moment when emotions turn

Proud

I reach above with outstretched timbered arms
The cloudless sky beats its heat
The days are long
Cool evenings a mirage

I impose my solitary ghostly grandeur
Contrasting against the distant purple-hazed hills
Not concealed by harsh red and ochre

When showers fall
Leaves will cover these seemingly brittle limbs
I'll be different
But ever remain the same

Worthless

I feel…

    like a piece of newspaper
    clipped for its importance
    discarded when the moment passes

Graveside

for my father – Aubrey Cecil Hannah

We thought we had so much time
The day before you passed

We shared so much
We shared so little
We'd only just begun

And now I sit and contemplate

> Whistling brings a cacophony of memories
> – hammering, sawing
> – your old glue pot filled to the brim with success
> – fine furniture, slick concrete paths and neat lawn edges
> – parties, prawns and judging sheets

In this place filled with plaques of heartbreak
A stillness of souls hover
Row upon row of remembrance
Red, yellow roses – plastic
Left to last between extended absence

I lay fresh flowers
It doesn't matter how long they last
> – only that I came
> – that I remembered

His heart was big
He used it to the limit

I Saw Beauty

White-as-snow countenance
Cherry-red lips
Sumptuous timeless kimono wrapping the mystery

Tip-toeing in wooden sandals
This geisha floats from person to person
Rising
Sitting
With the fluidity of steam from teacups

Whispering a confession of desire
To caress the strings of the *shamisen*
Perfect the music
Entertain
Please

Empowered to leave
Staying by choice
Rejecting ignorance of her worth
Showing gentility of spirit
Commitment
Guarding the secrets of the last 400 years

She pours the tea
I ask, 'Why a geisha?'
'I saw beauty,' she replied

Silence of Love

My heart beating to the thoughts of love
    knowing the day is coloured with soft joy

No fireworks
No applause
No adulation

Just a confidence of a happy ever after

I'm Here

I'm here
Here in the pit of my life
Like a slug
A snail, stomped on, not wanted

Here where Satan hunts for lost souls
Who've lost the ability to crawl out of the mire
No sun
No light
No promise
Or joy or happiness

Liquid gloom slurps across my shoulders
Oozes down the folds of sagging disappointment
Mud adheres, stays in dark limp hair
The taste of grime fills me with fear

Sewage of despair clings
I'm polluted with misery
Capability suffocated
Options drowned by relentless doubt

I'm here
Here, where I don't want to be
Like a refugee
A wanderer in a distant land

My fingernails dig into the wall
Scratch at possibilities
I grip the imaginary curb of tomorrow
I see light
I'm no longer there

I'm here
At last
With hope

Let Go

A gentle breeze whispers the serenity of autumn
A falling leaf brushes my shoulder with a message
Let go
Before life can begin again

Water

Drip
Drip
Drip
a leaky tap
the drain accepts the trickle

far away
in deepest Africa
that water
would save a child

Lucifer of Hate

I am Lucifer and the fire of hate is my power

Souls buckle as the flames of malice burns happiness
sucks oxygen from joy

I dance in celebration
Laughter bursts from my malevolent lungs, sprouting evil
I fan the embers of wickedness as the smoke curls around their doubts

But then I slip, fall flat with hope heavy on my back
An inferno reaches me, spawns across the criminal intent

The souls, smothered with cinders, gather courage

Tears from loved ones fall onto this hell and drown the blaze
Cleanses them
Washes me away

Noisy Contemplation

Don't stroll the path for quiet of hour
Amid gums and eucalyptus
For birds shatter the silence
With moments full of noise

Squawks and songs
Calls and caws
Tweets amid the branches

Don't stroll the path for quiet of hour
Amid gums and eucalyptus
For birds will break the silence
And uplift your soul with joy

Colour Me Black

The malignant hue reflects from the mirror
Covers me
Envelopes perception of my day

I see only discouragement
Feel only discontent

Carry pain with every step
And know no future without it

Colour me black today
For my world is monochrome
And I grieve hope

Beyond Remorse

The old bones of regret:
    of deeds carelessly done
    of spiteful actions holding intent
Lay across the joy and pain of memory

Liberate your future:
    of now
    of tomorrow
Find serenity beyond remorse

One Soul

In the depths of the blue blue darkness
a creature, at home in this expanse
opens itself as best it can
displays the entrapment of a fisherman's waste
hooked under an eye

A manta ray shares hopelessness
spreads wide its desperate wings
hovering above the diver
begging for relief

Sizing up each other
both wait
Reckoning on reciprocal courage
both wait

The diver ignores fear
flips his approach to the leviathan
reaches out with compassionate hands
removes the imbedded hook
one then two, then three

Satisfied with effort
he waits
Satisfied with liberation
it waits

In the depths of the blue blue darkness
they wait
respecting the encounter
they wait

Before departing to worlds apart
in an unbelievable moment
man and ray have one soul

Rodeo Riding

I fear for his life

Hours of training went into this performance
Hours and countless hours
Rodeo riding as an occupation requires strong muscle, sharp eye and raw courage
He endures long trips to far off places, solitary rooms, and restless sleep

Dawn announces it is time to strap on spurs and be ready for the fight

I fear for his life

An unbroken horse will rear, bolt
Scared beyond its life
Frightened beyond knowledge of man
Anxious to be rid of its burden

I fear for his life

He is dislodged
He lies still like a rag doll
Dust explodes around panicked hooves
They click inches from his head

I fear for his life

The horse whinnies as it's gathered by handlers
My man is lifted onto a stretcher
He acknowledges me with a fading smile, an uplifted thumb

A last the fear abates

The Old Woman

The old woman sleeps
The day is passing

The body wanes but not enough to creep into eternity
What use are the hands
What use are the feet

Tears won't ease the futility of wanting
To return to capability
To return to yesterday

Nothing can be done for this lingering soul
Only gentle caring
Only gentle loving

Memory persists in lighter moments
Sometimes it slips away
Sometimes it isn't there

The sun goes
The moon goes
The sun returns
The old woman sleeps on

Yesterday and You

The strings sing their melancholy music
My heart wanders to yesterday and you

The drifting notes touch and injure places of longing
I hear my soul tinkle on breaking
Like a triangle lost between staves

The strings sing their melancholy music
My heart wanders to yesterday and you
And tomorrow disappears

Whispering Hope

At the far reaches of Earth
From East to West
Across mountains, valleys, oceans and deserts
Through cities, villages and lonely corners
Are the hopes and dreams of the brave-hearted
The meek
Youth and the aged

Let not the dreams be shattered
   by the unwanted guest of
      FEAR
      HATRED
      GREED

Whisper hope to all hearts
Send wistful dreams to yearning souls
Bid clinging resistance
And endless persistence
For the brave-hearted
The meek
Youth and the aged

May hope reside
In the reaches of Earth
From East to West
And the distance between

Shadow of Me

The me of today,
    remembers yesterday,
        and the person I was then
            yearned for what might come

www.ingramcontent.com/pod-product-compliance
Lightning Source LLC
Chambersburg PA
CBHW062152100526
44589CB00014B/1798